To Jody

I hope you enjoy

FOOTFALLS

my Poems

XO XO

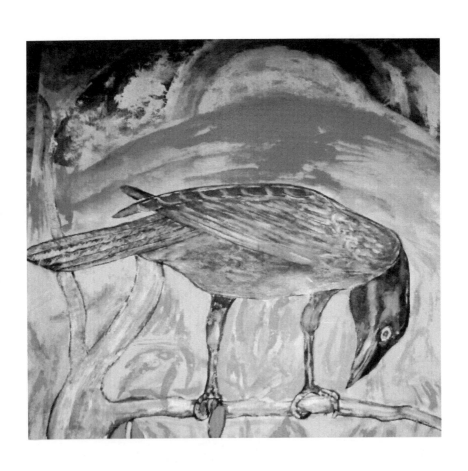

JAMES ERET

FOOTFALLS

POEMS

Esoterica Press   San Diego, CA

Designed and typeset by Esoterica Press
Front and back cover photos by Carolyn Werley

First Printing March 2015.

All inquiries and permission requests should be addressed to the publisher:

Esoterica Press
3559 Grim Avenue
San Diego, CA 92104
wrldtrvl@pacbell.net

Library of Congress of Congress Cataloging-in-Publication Data

Eret, James, 1948-
 [Poems. Selections]
 FOOTFALLS : Poems / JAMES ERET
     pages cm.
  ISBN 978-1-312-96301-6 (alk. paper)
I. Title.

ACKNOWLEDGMENTS

There comes a time in even the most reluctant poet's life when, after great hesitation, a book must be born, proof of a lifetime of effort. This volume represents a sampling, a randomly-curated collection.

The art on pages 9, 12, and 14 is by Motoko Kamada. I greatly appreciate her allowing me to use these gorgeous pieces. All other art work and photos are by James Eret.

I am grateful to the editors of the following publications, where these poems first appeared, sometimes in an earlier version:

Serving House Journal: Go Out with the Music Playing
Paterson Literary Review: In the August Heat
Spillway: Snowy Owl
Naugatuck River Review: Minefields
Blue Collar Review: Proposition 187
Midwest Quarterly: Suicide at Great Lakes Boot Camp
Canary: Winter Birds
Ibbetson Street Magazine: Odysseus
Del Sol Review: Words without Music
Avocet: Great Blue Heron
Iodine Poetry Journal: First Robins
Del Sol Review: The Well
Art of Being Human, Vol. I: Death at the Kabul Marketplace
Del Sol Review: My Landlord
The Art of Being Human, Vol. I: The Children of Terezin

City Works: La Contenta
San Diego Poetry Annual: Flight 182
Waymark Journal: How Poets Die: John Berryman's Jump
Annual Anthology, The Writing Center: Footfalls
Altered States, NAMI: Dresden

Mentors and inspirations in the poetry community include: Paul Carroll, Dorianne Laux, Joe Millar, Cate Marvin, William Luvaas, Doug Holder, Derrick Alger, Koon Loon, Steve Kowit, Jon Wesick, and Irene Siegel. I would like to thank the Centrum Foundation for the scholarship to attend the Port Townsend Writers Workshop.

I would like to acknowledge my family members and friends, all of whom have greatly inspired me. In particular, Michael Turner, Carolyn Mogovero, Michelle Scheurell, Dan Woodward, Chris Vannoy, Paul Stangeland, Fred Longworth, Ròger Aplon, Judy Reeves, and Gayle Bluebird deserve special mention.

CONTENTS

Footfalls

No terra firma
Absolutely *Terra Del Fuego,*

Yet never I a footfall
Upon a tossing and turning rice field,
Creeping off the coast of North Vietnam,
Instead my fate to labor upon a broiling deck

Of the U.S.S. Arlington, AGMR-2,
Sister ship of the U.S.S, Pueblo,
Spy ships shadowed by shark-like Russian trawlers,
Causing no harm, save a constant itch,
Netting for salty secrets.

Yet never I a footfall
Upon a tossing and turning rice field,
Five miles off the coast, the mountains loom
Beyond the blinking semaphore of the signal eyes of light,
So still, so electric, when the arc light flashes
As my ship creeps closer to death's dark land,
Closing the gap to qualify for combat pay,
The contrast between the sea surface and the sea bottom.

The Marianas Trench of anxiety breathing with the waves,
The difference between the microseconds
Of living and dying.
Sunset bleeds out to our wake
Into the backwash of history,
We receive through the Bitch Box, and the news is bad.

Terror enough here to bring home; yet throughout
The ship's air-conditioned guts what chaos unravels 1968.

With the assassination of Kennedy and King,
Mayor Daley's utterings
During the riots at the Democratic Convention--
"We are here to preserve *disorder*" —
And bludgeon the innocent marchers in Lincoln Park.

I remember thinking I am safer sailing
Off the coast of Vietnam than being back in Chicago and
enduring its wounded summer.

Yet never I a footfall
In my dreams always lingering off the coast of Vietnam,
Wandering for too long,
Like Odysseus for an ordered home
To return to, standing finally on a peaceful shore,

The gray and green mountains looking down upon
The land of endless fire.

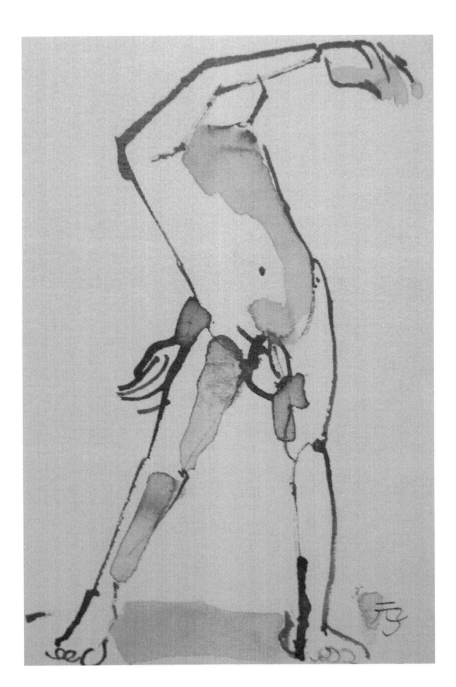

Suicide at Great Lakes Boot Camp, 1967

For Stephen Strawnchy

Sitting cross-legged,
In full-flower lotus,
He waits naked in the dark
Between the cool steel of the rails,
For the train to sound,
His bruised ears and ribs perk for the distant call
Coming closer for the kill.
Hounded beyond madness by the jarheads:
Kicks to his kidneys, bruises to his ego,
Taunting then tormenting at every turn,
He decides on this act of ultimate submission,
The final guttering of his spirit.
Now he faces the diesel of the night
And the promised freedoms of the abyss,
His last resigned screams wasted,
A mere whisper in the winter air
Beneath the weight of fire and final quietus
Of the insomniac wheels screeching flesh and blood.

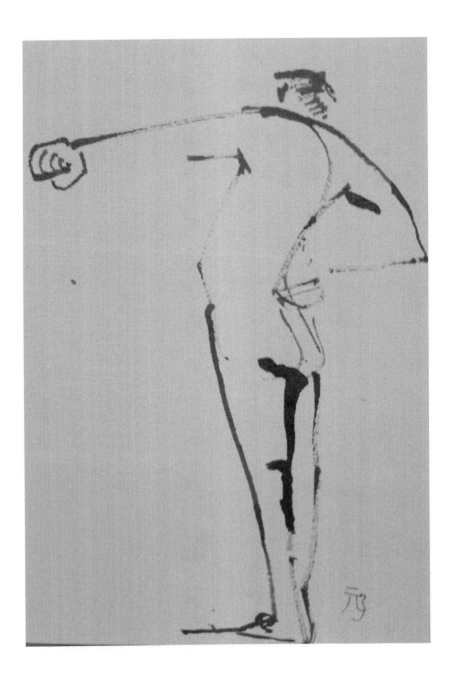

Chisel

"Who will walk with me into this terrible and beautiful
world?"   — Dorianne Laux

Looking down from the rocky fortresses, the imposing
parapets, in the crystal Valletta Harbor,
the dghajsas, the bum-boats as we called them,
Moored together in families of primary colors,
Sun-saturated and joyfully bobbing,
Laid-back lifestyle of Malta.

That eyeball staring at the sun too long,
Slashed with blood and veined 8-Ball hemorrhage.

The sailor, lone sentinel swiveled on the bar stool,
Knew we saw his injury but said nothing;
But so much anger burned in this orb.

Just how did you get that eye?

The White Mice, the Shore Patrol, did this to me.
At mail call I got a Dear John letter from my girlfriend.

He ascended the elevator from Hell
To the Garden of Hesperides,
Where the lovers strolled, hand-in-hand, made out,
Surrounded by the olive trees,
Those benevolent branches,
A quietus in King's Cross,
The sounds in the distance

Of bells and chanting Latin vespers.
So, filled with good tidings, he approached the precipice.
The idea was to finish his leap,
To die in Valletta, Malta,
Such an exotic and mysterious country.

The White Mice talked him down,
No ordinary drunk poised on the edge of the cliff,
His mistake to start cursing them back.

They did it with their night sticks,
While straightjacketed on a litter.
He told the White Mice to fuck themselves
And they thumped and thumped.
Blunt trauma bloat his evil eye.

Blind Homer, strumming your sad lyre, sing those songs,
That smell of lemons and olive trees,
Sea-surge of distant lovers,
Never again to walk, hand-in-hand.

The Children of Terezin: The Birth of Anxiety (Prose Poem)

"A total of around 15,000 children under the age of 15 passed through Terezin. Of these, around 100 came back."

What odd mother birthed Anxiety? What was her reaction when before she had ever known hate or love, only the will to survive, some fearful thought came tumbling out into the atmosphere? She survived on a distant plain with the wild beasts and she drew them with the blood of blueberries and charcoal, a bison on the wall of a cave, and she depicted her own beast charging in the damp stillness, among awed eyes, as the fire flickered out, and Fear, as high as ancient imagining could feel, piled up around the embers of hate, around another longing. O, there was almost hope, to be near their own kin, to seek out their mother in the darkness, to be nurtured in their starvation and their fear, these children in the pitch black, frozen at the sounds of the rolling thunder storms, wild winds, distant howlings of the beasts. For one instant, replaced by relief that they would endure one more day that they would survive another hour in the wilderness, when all was wilderness, but they knew instinctively that hate prowled the plains and what weapons, what thoughts, could stop it? Who were these predators? The light of the last embers went out. The children, eyes burning from the cave smoke, sought the comfort of their mother, but there were too many children. Countless children, innocent armies of children had to be sacrificed to the beast that roamed the plains, unchallenged.

The Minefields

"There are women who inspire you with the desire to
conquer them and to take your pleasure of them; but this one
fills you only with the desire to die slowly beneath her gaze."

Charles Baudelaire

I was asked to draw her portrait.
When we traveled to meet her in the flesh
I was flabbergasted by the beauty
in the sad eyes blinking before me.
Our mission, as if we needed a mission,
to visit with her and help her out of a fix.

We arrived at her "place," near the ocean boardwalk.
She was holed up in a motel room with her boyfriend.
They put their groceries in the dresser drawers
and cooked on a hot plate. Neither had a job.
I kept thinking, where does the money come from?
She was in the "Adult Entertainment Industry."
Who was I to condemn anyone?
So her mother, the nurse, gave her a supply of horse pills —
"Take these and try to stay out of harm's way."

This is a dark world with too many evil detours
leading down a path fraught with pitfalls at each turn,
on the lamb from the law, missing her hearing,
her boyfriend busted with a nickel bag?

How far can she travel from her mother
who would show her the precarious route to safety,
And steal her away from the tawdry
detonating breakers of the Pacific?

This is the way of the world:
be satisfied to be alive under such duress,
hide any remaining humanity,
and sell your beauty to those frothing pigs
who travel with darkness in their back pockets.

Be content to survive your creeping addictions,
this way of daily life you have and have not chosen;
it's in the genes; it's your tragic history,
mine canary of an impenetrable labyrinth,
no longer glowing with love of life,
too far gone in the darkness.

I ask myself, how can I draw this portrait?
My devils, which are real, must reside
on another side of the River Styx
from this young woman's,
this lost soul, whose face already bears
the cracks and crevices of a life lived in the minefields.

My Landlord   (The Apartment in Chicago)

To Bill Avrin--friend and poet

He sees nothing except grasping
Fingers, colorless Polish fields.
A great cold has swept through
His wiry body and he suspects
The packed train
Is leading to the bright Boneyard.

He is still strong, he still longs
For the finer things, his family
Is still together in the boxcar.
He watches the stark winter trees
Of Poland, the clicking and the clacking
Of the wheels, the smell of woolen coats
And urine not so bad because it is winter.

He still believes in an afterlife.

...No afterlife

Yet I am here in Chicago,
Fifty years after those events
That has turned the color of photo negatives
In my mind...and I never want them developed —
But year-by-year they rise up,
Up from the bloody fields
Of the Boneyard.

How did I handle this?
How can I own property?
I treated my tenants like I was treated
In Auschwitz---when they most need heat
I deny them heat, when they thirst I make them
Beg for water, I let the roaches rule the rooms,
And I will destroy the invasion of insects with the
Most foul-smelling bug-killing agent;
In a frenzy of killing, I murder them
By the millions, their brown bodies
Quiver and run from the cracks and the crevices.

I see my face in the mirror and it looks
Permanently melted, the color drained,
Waxen (how the hell did I survive?)
No matter that a mere dozen here suffer at my hands.
When millions suffered where I was long ago,
When the hanged ones
Danced the death dance.
A few survived--they couldn't kill us all--
But I will always fear the sound and sight
Of the goose-step,
Yet I can't do it myself; I'm caught in a permanent shuffle,
Trying to keep the wooden clogs on my feet--
You didn't dare lose them.
It feels like my toes have been fused together--
On the coldest days I rub them to feel
The simple feeling of warmth, of being lucky
To be alive.

I was cast ashore in many countries.
I had no name

Save this faded blue number of five digits
Tattooed to my right forearm, under the skin,
The fish of death
In a winter pond —

        Ach, the guards are gone.

I cannot smile anymore and my tenants accuse me
Of being an asshole, an unfeeling bastard,
The concertina rolls of barbed wire catching birds
In mid-song on nervous mornings when I knew
I would never get out alive--and I still feel that way.

I see smoke billowing over Chicago snowdrifts,
Rising and falling into flesh ditches
That fertilizes new grass, seedlings green with memories
Of the day-to-day dying and survival
Of the Boneyard.

Crusoe's Prayer

Inspired by Luis Bunuel's *Adventures of Robinson Crusoe*

Alone at 3 am in February
Surrounded by an unknown island,
Long ago abandoning the shipwreck
That once stranded me here
After half-circling the watery globe,
Only to be tossed like a toy
Into the open mouth of the sheltering harbor.
A long sadness overtakes me.

I decide to climb the highest mountain
On this island, to orient myself,
Not just in a geographical sense.
What I need is a geography of the spirit,
A way to make my loneliness more palatable.
On the summit, cloud-high,
Competing with the cries of the gulls,
I fiercely rant the 23rd Psalm,
So that my words might branch out
And echo as multitudes of phantom men,
Vanquishers of my solitude
To fill the folding canyons
With sibilant syllables carried aloft
Above the still waters misting at my feet.

I do not want this, to be a castaway
Dressed in goat-skin rags, an animal with no dignity.
Where is the human connection,
The need in my heart's journey,
For a compass rose to flower, to show me the way home?
Panicking, I sprint down
From the palm-covered heights
To the seashore and there run madly,
Mimicking the nervous agitation of the sandpipers.
Then I deeply envision a footprint,
Maybe nothing, maybe Man Friday.
I continue to be this island's solitary shepherd.
Rumors of rescue painfully curl in the waves.
They say the sea has no memory.
I shall not want.

Go Out With the Music Playing

Go out with the music playing.
Never give up.
Go past all illusions
to a place where the source
of the River Styx is a mere trickle,
walk down the riverbank
and slippery rocks where
the river's pulse reaches a crescendo,
then slows to an inexorable stop.
Hear the sound of the creaking oarlock
of the river rower, Charon, seen distant
in the fearful mist
as he journeys toward you
to gather his alms.
Now the skeleton comes to claim
you and turn you to one of his own
by ferrying you across the river
to a shore where the muses mourn.
We love you: as you fight to the death,
delirious on morphine, you try to sing
your beloved arias from the Rosenkavalier.
Go out with the music playing.
You entered this world to music.
Music gave you sustenance and you gave music substance.
Now music gives to you again,
a blissful respite from the marauding cancer cells
which will soon silence your melody.
Linger, linger, linger!
with us a little longer

and keep open your Delft-blue eyes,
which dance at every note,
whether sharp or flat,
for whatever time is left.
Go out with the music playing.

The Forgotten Soldier at My Lai

He was normal, just an average grunt,
Like so many nameless raw recruits dressed in green,
Until that fateful hump into a foul rice paddy,
Smelling of shit, and the almost relieved feeling
Of red mud squishing between his toes,
That maybe the earth itself would suck him down below
The great heaving water buffalo wallowing
In the barely-breathed gnat-swarmed air.
His next step blew him airborne
As the toe-popper exploded.
All his senses were blown away.

One leg was shredded and the other sheared off.
For a microsecond, he remembered what it was like
To stride the earth on two feet.
He screamed but couldn't hear his own cries,
The blast concussion piercing his ear drums like a lance
His writing hand was blown off;
This he didn't see for he was also blinded by the blast.
He was evacuated by chopper;
During the dust-off his heart stopped and was restarted
By medics who hit him with a syrette of morphine.

His heart stopped five times.
His heart was restarted five times.
It was a miracle he was alive.
He could talk,
Yet could not hear his own voice echo into the void.
Who would love him when he returned to the World?

"I am almost home. I am almost alive."
In the unfamiliar darkness, somewhere
Among the sounds, kisses await him.
In his drugged state,
He limps to the direction that once, before his deadly step,
Was the light, was the light of home.

Words Without Music:
While Stationed in Vietnam, 1968

Gear-grinding words
Words thrown at the teeth and shattering there
    Sacred mounds and altars of words in holy places
Words that shine like wings of grackles in the sunlight after
    rain showers
Words that build with their hands any form of survival
    new temples that are carefully constructed with memories
Words standing below the lakes on stilts in muddy
    floodwaters pouring life into the ubiquitous paddy fields
Words pounding the shores with the agony of ravenous gulls
Words churning in the sand restless regions of the ocean
Words speechless a start with no endings
Words that kiss the breeze with a nervous laughter
Words with far country cries and unturned eyes that whisper
Words with no wisdom only terror
Words gliding like zigzag bats, rabid
Words like white with newness day's innocence dies fast
Words that kiss you sweetly when you're through
Words that soothe and warm your bones
Words, wet monsoon words, rolling thunderously
Words trickling down your dry palate
Words of distant torrential winters blowing ice
Words of legendary storms ocean-lashing tsunamis
Black hole words silver words muttering around the green
    upheaval mountains entrapped by fire and mystery
Prevailing words
Die-cast words like clouds across the stars into destinies
Soft spray of sun shower words and sweat of insect words

Words of meaning of unopened letters
Words of the black and empty boxes
Words that dry up without a sound
Words with raw flesh ripped out
Words of waterfalls, star-shaped words
Dancing moon words, iron blood words
Words for the wind
Great armies of words like ants advancing into the unknown
    which is omnipresent
Tongue-busting words
Words of fire
Words of arguments with the drunken midnights
Words, fearful words, like lovers who touch and disappear
Words spitting rapid fire
Monkey screeching words
Words of far and holy and unsightly visions lifting in rings of
    painted smoke
Ear-splitting words
Words of walking wounded home
Words of the multitudes
Words of the last footfalls that begin at each click of the tired
    heal on stones
More words than lost arms to carry them in
Temple words growing solemn with serpents
    In the smoking ruins of words

On the Closing of San Onofre Nuclear Plant

For Taro Aizu, survivor of nuclear "mishaps"

Beyond the Pacific beaches
The blind rip tides try to shake
Off their bruises as it is always done.

Taro Aizu, who haunts Mt Fuji's triangular shadow,
As the word grinds off its axis,
Past glories are now quixotic dreams
Empire ended by the horror of man-made fission.

The building many called
"The Two Tits," nipples erected
In the cool sea air, will shut down.

San Onofre, silenced nuclear plant,
Some brave souls complain of your closing
Cheap energy, but at what price?

Already, the detritus of Japan's tsunami
Has drifted to our unclean shores.
Now ghost ships settle down in the lapping surf
Devoid of their captains.

The two maimed nuclear reactors
Are joined by that vast Pacific
I once crossed, Japan to Hawaii
As my atom splitting vessel tracked the Apollo 10.
A hero's welcome for the astronauts,

Angry protests instead for the conscripted crew.
So now we are linked in our laments.

Yet, Taro Aizu smiles in the wreckage.
There, on contaminated Fukishima soil
He plants seedlings
Of cherry trees which might thrive,
Given a chance, given a chance.

Dead Homeless Man

"He has a history of turning down services." County Mental
Health Service Report on John Doe

1-25-98

Death descends, not always spectacular like in war,
battle on a global scale, millions rubbed out...,
One lonely man, staggering from the ER,
steel nipples unhooked from some EKG machine,
still pasted where the heart's pulse
vanished, quiver full of arrows,
on the storm-gray porch where I work,

This ragamuffin man had wandered
from off the map, one out of the multitudes,
onto this weathered porch of rotten wood.
The front door is locked.
The key to it, shaped pyramidal and golden,
Broadcasts its own death rattle.
Yet the lifeless body would not be stirred.

A coagulated pool of blood,
the size of my hand, dried on the gray stairs,
blood clotted in the saturated
mouth and bushy mustache,
whiskering to its tips in stone grayness,
after a death stagger and then silence.

Setting aside my fear,
I picked up the dirty, cadaver's right forearm,
searching in vain for the pulse of life.
The cops finally came with their forms
to fill out; the corpse had no ID, John Doe.
The paramedics teathered a machine
to the cadaver's awaiting metal nipples.
No spark of life, no heroic measures
to save this anonymous one from death.
Lazarus would not rise this afternoon in January,
No miracle for no-name.

This dusty wanderer died,
unmourned on my gray island of memory.
on this Super Bowl Sunday.
As Denver beat Green Bay 31-24,
This Gray Man rushed into my heart,
clotting my memories--the entire porch
paradoxically more alive than ever before.
His energy lost, his years lost, yet energy
flowed between the two of us,
much more than the Super Bowl could generate,
for I still had my energy tilting off its axis,
as they zipped his sad ass into a body bag and rattled
him on the metallic-sounding gurney that ushered him
into the Underworld he knew all too well.

Flight 182 San Diego (1984)

A wounded jet, colliding with a
Small Cessna, dipped wing aflame,
Dives down to certain destruction
In a residential area.
Flesh falls, plowing through bricks
With superhuman speed--
"A No Survivor Crash."
Fire and smoke rise from the rubble.
Two miles away my family lives
In a run-down apartment with a cactus garden,
Safe from the site of the crash.
We are too numbed by tragedy,
By the separate sheets that cover separate body parts.
We have fallen in love with disasters,
The horrible details,
As long as they are not our limbs
That have been torn asunder
Penetrating the walls of our neighbors.

Dark Waters -- How Poets Die

> In a dark time the eye begins to see... Theodore Roethke

I.   The Glass House

He was our poet of the "spirit," one of his favorite words.
Spirit in the sense of even the smallest living things such as
Jade-colored moss under the massive glass dome in Saginaw,
Michigan, where his Teutonic father had his own brutal Eden.
Papa Roethke, when not sprinkling the orchids, was yelling
German curses at his pudgy son, waltzing him around
The kitchen with his wife as an impotent referee.
What kind of pentameter did Ted learn from those soiled
knuckles scraping his head after his father had planted new
cuttings all day?

Something must have survived the Glass House--beauty and
fear: Fear of beauty and a manic sadness dogging him to his
dying days.

II.   Handcuffed in Poetry Class

He was a great poetry teacher by most accounts,
Yet not without his problems as when his massive energy
Went into overdrive during one class. The police
Were called and hauled him off in handcuffs
In front of his startled students, who said that as a group
They felt soiled by the experience, witnessing their mentor
Lugged away through the dusty hallways, wondering
whether he would return from that dark world of the mind to
teach again.

III.   Death Swim

For a big man, Ted Roethke was good athlete,
A tennis coach, and a fine swimmer. During breaks
In his teaching (for he never stopped composing verse),
He would brave the northwestern waves alone.
Years removed from the Glass House, the poetry awards,
Drinking bouts, and his battles of the spirit,
He went swimming in a friend's backyard pool.
They found him dead, bobbing face first in the water.
His large voice silenced.   The spirit drained.
The roots of his past split asunder during his heart attack,
Lighter than dandelion seeds, filling and falling in the air.

Massacre in a Wheatfield

When death circled the wheat field,
the corpses lay stiff,
their limbs intertwined
with the harvest.
Mythologies all over the globe
celebrate the sacredness of the circle,
the certainty and shape of the seasons,
rituals of the golden harvest.
This was supposed to be a healing field,
a cessation of all deep and ancient hostilities;
alas, blood revenge cuts too deep.

Vincent Van Gogh's last painting
before he mortally shot himself
was of crows hovering over a wheatfield,
his depression and deep anxiety slashed
in ponderous impasto strokes,
a vision so deep and weighty
that some art historians say
even today all the paint on his canvases
has not completely dried.
Someone else who has survived the purges
must try to finish the final harvest.
The blood there never seems to dry.

We are no peacekeepers.
We love war.

Proposition 187

Believe there are barriers
and not just between borders.
Hatred runs deep in the shadows.
It is our modern gospel.
We dream about a fabled place.
We want to enter our dreams
for many reasons, get close
enough to see the magic city of lights.
Yet we arrive there, only to have the dream denied,
hardened by hardships.
What is accomplished by these mad dashes
across the perilous landscapes,
searchlights in pursuit all the way?
Jesus and Maria never had a chance.
They lived like shadows,
fragmented and empty,
lusting for the land of Milk and Honey,
found freedom tasting like salt,
knee-deep in egrets, white as clouds.
Tonight there is a resplendent, yet stark beauty
to the moon's rising over the peaks
of the unjudging mountains.
The moon, no pompous lawmaker,
blesses their journey, lighting
the way like the suicidal moths,
pinging again and again at the light.
Even those who make it safely,
after all that sprinting around
the checkpoints, handcuffed to something

baser than their pride, learning that the place
they dreamed of is no better than
the place they left. They feel angry,
bashing at the moon
like a smirking piñata,
full of sweets and broken promises.

Dresden

I walk out under a firestorm sun to
smell the shrubs and the last blossoms.
Washed out and receding dreams are left behind.
One was of my mother limping toward me
on her one good knee, arthritic spores filling the air,
her flesh slowly sliding off her bones,
her once strong Teutonic frame.
Father burns with cancer nodes
and seeks the deep shade of the pepper trees.
His failing heart causes him to sweat like a sea.
At work, at UPS, after hours of loading boxes
off a conveyor belt, a boring river of rubber,
I feel a fever coming on, a deep hatred for manual labor
and every zip code in the entire state of Wisconsin
that I have been forced to memorize.
Bill collectors are more persistent than cockroaches.
I want to burn the daily mail and unplug my telephone.
My body and my mind are spinning out of control
as I drive home in the midnight darkness.
Just when the last anxiety attack ceases and I feel
some safety, that everything around me, within me,
Is working in a tenuous balance, I hear a massive drone
emerging overhead from the gray cloud formations,
promising an unexpected rain of fire falling and engulfing
everything I treasure: my family, my health, my home,
my fantasies, my always beloved rivers.
One after another, loved, cherished, each a sacred object,
is torn from me, the last defenses destroyed.
There and there and there I am eye-to-eye
with the unspeakable destruction of Dresden.

Death at the Kabul Marketplace

I awoke to the wails of the muezzin wafting
From the minaret. On the mountains,
Layers of fog masked the fir forests.

I awoke to the calls from the horn of plenty,
Seeds planted in my memory.
Today's sun shines on market day.

Forgetting the fire and fear of those slayers
Of my sleep, my sons and daughters,
I haggled for fruits and fares.

Arcing from the mountains came produce
No one bargained for, let loose
From the mists that always hide a truce.

I awoke, hearing shrapnel burst and fly
Around me like a mad festival, the brooding
Mountain peaks silently soaking up

More of the feuding history of my blood.
I awoke and haggled for fruit and my life and lost.

Snowy Owl

"It is not more surprising to be born twice than once;
everything in nature is resurrection." — Voltaire

Her husband returned back as a Snowy Owl.
He perched with his prey, a grey squirrel,
Draped over an oak limb burdened with snow,
The owl's talons bleeding into the limbs.
Slowly swiveling his chalky face,
He scanned the dark forest behind him,
His sleepy but deadly gold eyes missing
Nothing that breathed in the back acres of those woods.
He called gently in the falling snowflakes.
He noticed his wife, only twenty feet away,
Peering at him through the window,
Her binoculars enlarging his bloodied talons
And golden, ghostly eyes.
He did not know he was back
As he opened his wide wings,
Unfolding another lifetime of memories
And returned forever into the dark haws,
His silent wings beating like her pulse,
Slowing to barely a trickle.

Great Blue Heron

What does it mean to be a great thing?
Does it mean that you dream some great discovery,
One that would set you spinning awake
Like a shining top of sunlight
To illuminate for you
The perfect workings of the world?
Like the wisest of philosophers
There you would stand, staring in front of you,
Though a slim creature,
For one pure moment, balanced on a skinny leg.
By the greatest of gifted knowledge
You could lift a blue-feathered dream
Hundreds of feet above the estuaries,
And only then, only then,
Would you understand the majesty of your making,
Your destiny to wander, alone,
Looking into the immense passion that is the sun,
While you spread your wide wings
And large shadow over the nervous swamp?

17-Year Locusts

"You could see waves of sound rising in the air." Emma Eret

There was a premonition of a plague in the air, a vague,
Yet unrelenting, feeling of being overwhelmed by summer.
After a long, long sleep, the locust crawled

Out of the darkened crannies of the earth,
Overly anxious to burst into song when they felt
The glimmer of their first summer sunlight.

With their crystalline wings beating beyond measure,
They smothered everything in their path with a rasping,
Their cicada decibels rising to unimaginable levels.

Assaulted by crescendo after crescendo,
The adults among us were dazed in a din of disbelief.
The children, more amenable to this strange onslaught

Were in paradise, joyfully stomping on the brittle bodies
And stuffing the hapless insects greedily into their air rifles
To shoot randomly at each other.

Grandfather returned from his small orchard,
Where these unwelcomed visitors had ravaged his fruit trees,
Overpowering each and every apple, peach, and pear.

The birds battled the black manna in the treetops,
On every limb, even in mid-air, in skirmish after skirmish;
An avian feast of epicurean proportions

Until the birds were barely able to lift away in flight.
The cicadas' songs mounted to a final, chaotic climax,
For in one last freakish quarrel with the elements,

The sky grew sick and seemed to vomit out this excess.
The mass of dead wings tangled, glittering on the ground
Had been the sounds of a million tambourines.

Although this dark hoard did not strip every bit of green
They crawled upon every neuron of each of our minds.
Their echo reverberates as a harbinger for the next generation.

First Robins

After the Midwest thunderstorms and the gridlock hum of traffic
Had been silenced, the thunderheads migrated
Like great white beasts, leaving debris of soft sounds,
Dripping water draining into the green grasses of northern Illinois.
A thousand pools of raindrops rang out,
Feathered lightly by a morning wind.
I was there on creation morning
With a hundred robins yanking up earthworms
And singing their red songs from a sodden field.

Ten years later, well aware of my own shattered dreams,
Walking under the broad shoulders of Orion,
I think of those robins of Illinois.
I remember the morning
In spring, looking at the robins hopping
Gingerly in the field of memory that will always be there,
Then the feelings of that day return in a deluge,
Being alone in the desert, this parched place.
Can it be endured, somehow accepted?

How Poets Die: John Berryman's Jump

Demons nest in the long gray beard
And a small bird, with no progeny,
Sits on broken blue eggs.
Minnesota: waterways and haunting loon songs.
Too much book-learning, high-strung senses, what
Reasons, Mr. Bones, what reasons for the leap-swirl?
What reasons to be killing oneself,
In the same state where father blew his brains out?
Tumbling off the edge of the bridge after a salute,

Calling for Kate, my young wife,
My thick glasses flying off before I hit
The riverbank and the cold surge. Sober days
Did it. I can't take all this clean living,
Falling off the wagon, then back on, now falling
Foolishly off the bridge. I saw Dylan Thomas die,
The bloody bastard never woke
After guzzling a Welsh pyramid of straight whiskeys.

Now follow him to his dominion, Death.
Swirling last, still thinking — amazing--
Still thinking all the way down to the broken bones,
Trying to conjure up a last line,
The iambic rhythm of the river driving me
Into the shadows under the bridge,
Swept along, floating in a thick sweater and coat.
Bullets of darkness. I knew it, Mr. Bones,
And who on earth would have guessed,
That life would all end like this, falling
Like Icarus. Where are my wax wings, Mr. Bones?
Someone is dredging the riverbank,
Someone has found me in a sodden pile,
Gray and worthless as an old stinking truck tire.

Death hurts, Jack. Death hurts.
The river flows on without me.
The last things I saw sober
Were the barn swallows flashing in the sun.
They were gulping, in a feeding frenzy,
The insects that were swarming over me.

Always Finding the Moon

No matter how overcast the sky,
my youngest son always finds the moon,
pointing like he has just discovered it,
full of youthful excitement, saying "It burns."
As children grow such discoveries become rare;
They face the loss of innocence and
encounter death for the first time.

It is gloriously overcast today
as we drive past a field of dead sunflowers,
slashing over the puddles and bumpy roads.
From a meandering gray haze in the east, rising
like a dream over the restless Lake Michigan waters,
a full moon appears, disappears, then appears again.
My youngest son points his rigid index finger
into the eye of The Sea of Tranquility.

Before lunar silence pulls the final tidal blanket
over a once deep-remembered, magnetic night,
a Luna moth, in its sacred greenness hidden from the view
of mere mortals, flies at the light of the moon, sporting
such delicately beautiful, ribbed, verdant and veined wings,
perfectly camouflaged--flitting through a darkened meadow
like a phantom, like my son's unbridled imagination,
all our imaginations, when we choose to use them.

Together these moonlit visions, our Luna moths,
dance till dawn by the light in its fullness,
by the cathedrals of the moonlight.

Chicago Locusts

What do I say to the young boy
from a local street gang
who has brought me the husk
of a dead locust,
feather-light and headless?
This insect's song is gone
and soon his kin will also be silenced,
marking the end of this once-in-a-childhood event.

High and low, hidden in the foliage,
wings vibrate with a shimmering rasp
that rises and defines the season's heat,
a humidity of wild music and a chorus
in memory of this year,
alive, yet living on borrowed time.

The young boy from the projects
who proudly displays his discovery
tells me he keeps a live one
at home, in a jar, where it
lullabies him to sleep in the slum.

This summer in Chicago is sizzling,
with the pent-up energy of unrequited youth,
yet in spite of this humidity,
the locusts sing their sarcastic songs
in the honey-combed trees of tenements.

I dream of a brute beauty of unlimited water,
an incessant sea of sound,
an endless source of wonder for this boy,
who is destined to be gunned down
in an alley by a rival gang.

The locusts seem impervious to it all,
their mad songs unrelenting,
in tribute to all of our short lives,
to the glory of living on the edge,
until their tree symphonies fade out
into autumn, their husks remaining,
and their heads fall off.

In the August Heat

Knowing not grieving remembers a thousand savage and
lonely streets.   William Faulkner, *Light in August*

In the August heat, dreams freshly minted,
I rekindle part of my past, my boyhood,
on the football field.
The excitement of the crowd going mad
and the thump of the marching band bass drum,
a strong and steady heartbeat of immortal energy.

In the August heat, dreams are a harbinger,
I wonder what my future will bring.
New memories lit by my lover's smile,
Splayed across the bed.
Yet so many memories lost and fading,
Piece-by-piece, my mind losing hold as the body ages.

In the August heat, dreams dying down,
I try to see the distant peak covered
with pure snow and there reach
a balance in my life, past and future--
the world, good and bad, to the bone.

MRI Test

Shake and bake me
wake me after unloading me
from the million-dollar coffin
engulfing me with the loud, tapping
sounds of hidden hammers,
percussionists in an erstwhile military march.

I lay perfectly still, a soldier at attention,
hands folded with frozen fingers,
cool metallic noises, battering rams
sending me over the edge of sanity.
Put me in the freezer to cool me down,
water in the ice tray, waiting to solidify.
Cabin fever infects my mind.

The voice behind the booth is sparse, soporific.
Why does she stand behind the glass booth,
softly giving directions, twirling dials?
Will my magnetic mind point to the north,
steadying up under the machinations of machines?

Even the most rousing jazz buzzing
through the headphones is a paltry distraction.
Miles Davis would do fine if not drowned out by my fear
and the wild shaking resonance of this tunnel
mining the treasures of my mind,
the Mother Lode of all the fortunate, healthy ones.

Soon the cranial gems will be glittering on slides
to be interpreted as a weird history of my head.
Dark to light, wrestling with the urge to swallow
as I am flooded by a great river of light,
my health a mysterious jigsaw puzzle to be solved.
Hours, or was it just moments, later
my distracted doctor flipped her chart and declared:

Mister Eret, the results are negative;
they found nothing in your head.

As my family and friends have always said.

The Pact

I have an unofficial pact with my two sons:
that if I suffer a stroke or if my senses
fail me and I am unable to orient myself,
to recognize what city or planet I am on,
wheel me up into the mountains,
maybe the majestic Sierras, and leave me there.

While my family's Catholic desire may be
to stuff me like a Thanksgiving turkey
and display my trussed-up body at a wake,
I prefer to go out in greater style, without fear.
So, if a mountain lion approaches me in curiosity
while I am pissing in my drawers, in helpless humility,

I will say:

> *Come over here, honey.*
> *Tired of being haunted by hunters*
> *and indignant citizens killing you off,*
> *one-by-one into needless extinction?*
> *Come over here and dig in,*
> *with all the strength of your sand-colored fur,*
> *tooth and claw, devour me,*
> *and lend a final dignity to my brittle bones.*

Island / When Life is Over

There is a man-made island
in the middle of a man-made pond
with a plank-log bridge
to traverse the long grasses.
The frog spawn foams,
the tadpoles emerging in dark clouds
of madly-swimming tails.

It is a bulldozed creation,
gouging an ovoid wound
into the damp earth of the swamp
as long-buried arrowheads rise to the surface.
Green herons hide amongst the dead branches,
sticking out like hollow, dark fingers.
On the island, one weeping willow brushes the pond surface.
A lone paper birch leans out,
shadowing the duckweed detritus.
The remaining fish forage
for the whirligigs that swim in endless circles
and water striders skate magically
on the murky surface while the blue darners reflect
the color of the shimmering summer sky.

Bare-chested, eyes closed,
My father slumps in a canvas chair
on a catamaran he made,
the pontoons drifting aimlessly.

He nods as the sunlight burns his bald head,
thoughts drifting toward some resplendent vision.
He lets his mind and body flow as one
with the insects and the water birds.
He wonders if this is what it is like
when life is over.

The Well

I go to the well for water,
the purest water in the world,
for me in that moment
A wooden bucket is
full and sloshing over
with a cool wetness of dreams dying
and resurrection of another thirst.
I cup my hands like in reverse prayer
and hold a handful of water
drawn from the depths.

I don't know what this well is,
real or imaginary; I know I taste
the water and drink a little.
My thirst is so great that I could drink an ocean,
drink every drop from this source
though I feel it is endless
extending downward
like a damp root with dark music,
running into the underworld
few of us know in the bright sunlight.

As I look back at my life and its longings,
I splash handful after handful of water on my face,
not caring what gets wet or that the spillage
I share with the grass and the weeds
accidentally makes them green again.

O, there is suffering that has no bounds;
strangers come forth to this well
to call my name which echoes down
and mixes with the depth.
It could be my last day feeling the thirst
and slaking it and I light up with
the smile of a king who has found his realm
and rules with special powers, special riches.

Odysseus

A familiar feeling comes
when one is not really home,
when dumb-struck by the freezing winds.

Fear crams feverishly into every crevice,
every pore and shadow,
the meadows barren around the estate.

Battle it out, a Trojan War,
blowing back and slashing over the sea
with a power of angered gods.

The new self is hidden,
the lost years piling up in pyres
of my fallen friends.

Every night of my absence,
Penelope unravels the tapestry on her soft loom,
to trick the suitors and win her more time.

Once free of my fate from wandering in the known world,
I bend the great bow in the hall of my ancestors
and so as to not tempt fate, I kill every suitor in the great hall,

washing their blood off my warrior's hands,
finally reunited with my wife,
two strangers staring at the gnarled olive tree.

Shield

I stumbled into Friend to Friend Clubhouse,
in downtown San Diego, to teach my first art class to the
homeless.
To pass through its portal, I quickly found a hole
through a bickering bunch of ragamuffin men
who were drunkenly arguing on the sidewalk outside.
While I waited for the class to begin, a solitary woman
was cautiously creeping into a corner behind me.
She muttered, to no one in particular, save the listener of
unheard fear--
Those men outside are searching for Crack Heaven.

A great straining quiver rippled across her face
as if she had been attacked by moray eels.
She augured that someone outside on the sidewalk
was going to get killed and go to their version of paradise.
She collapsed into a ball and played possum in my shadow,
her eyes terrorized, half-hidden by her shaking hands.
Her entire body seemed beyond the hope of help
as I pondered this unexpected prelude to my new
assignment.

For a few minutes out of her twenty-four hours of fear
I was her shield against those wild and warty souls
who had, moments ago, tried to make her an unwilling
passenger in their perverse quest for Crack Heaven.
Her eyes assured me that such a place existed.

La Contenta

After the quickie marriage and divorce of 2004,
I thought back to when I was ten years old.
Blood red scarlet leaves
Were strewn around me as I hiked along
The Little Calumet River, polluted even then,
The forests haunted by hobo camps and
The hot blood of young lovers.
In the distance I could see the churning plume
Of white hot steam billowing
From a coal black locomotive.

Maybe I only dreamed this dark dragon of energy,
Yet this phantom train

Fueled my imagination like no other living thing.
I thanked the powers that created me for the gift
Of being alive to such possibilities.

Tower of Strength, blazing stars shooting
Over the spiky Joshua Trees that were like Grecian columns
Holding up the heavens and row after row after row
Of mountains with their gathered mists.

Tower of Strength, sidewinders, cold-blooded, slithered
Across the sunlit path on rocks that glittered like diamonds in
the daylight.
Immense distances, blazing azure, salmon-pink,
And always a lemon-light blanketing
The entire widening, hawk-hovering horizon.

Tower of Strength, you were not ventured from home,
Mingling out there with the slayers of the night.
You trekked to all the welcome places,
Passing aromas of creosote, mesquite, and juniper until
You arrived at a place not marked on any map.

You journeyed into that unknown region
You finally could call Home.

The Wintering Birds

My aunt is weary, knowing
in the biology of her bones
that at eighty-four the leaking heart valves
will shut down soon. She dreads
that final wrinkling
of her natural organism,
a process she has studied long and well,
teaching us the fine-tuning
of the green kingdoms.
Every time she ascends her hill,
the lace-delicate valve opening and closing,
the gates of her blood
falter and remind her
of the weakness of her flesh,
the way age comes on like a Midwest blizzard blowing
in its crystalline beauty and brutality.
Hidden predators hibernate in dead cherry wood logs.
Their pulses slowly lift their lungs.
She rests too often and with restless sleep.
Snowbound, she watches, for the last time,
the wintering birds,
the blood-red cardinals stabbing
at the sunflower seeds in the feeder,
dangling by a thread
above the deeply-frozen snow.

Wristwatch

Sweeping its hands
mortal bracelets
unstoppable

Without anxious eyes
erased memories
face with no emotions

Big and little hands
the hare and the tortoise
who will win

Is the tick a breath
gorged with tiny gears
follows the fake heartbeat

Metallic, robotic, jagged wheels
part of your skin may not belong
tomb-saver, talk to me
as you wind with a flick of a wrist

Stop the world spinning on its axis
those men of the train
commuters through turnstiles
for the big bucks

Give in to your fire
gearing contest
clasp or unclasp your shackles.

The Palliative Ward

My flesh began unto my soul in pain,
Sicknesses cleave my bones;
Consuming agues dwell in ev'ry vein,
And tune my breath to groans. –George Herbert

The morphine drip is driving me crazy.
You would think I would be inured by now –
as my dying wife twists and turns the tubes
that set off the damned alarm one more time.
We have learned how to reset it
without calling and recalling the shift nurse
and leave tangled the rest.
The waiting is the worst time I have spent anywhere.
Has the outside world forgotten about her? About us?

Cathy is leaving us and fades in and out of sleep,
Wrestling each night with horrific anxiety attacks.
Her mouth is agape; I can hear the air forced down
its life-saving path like a silent, stalking visitor.
Each night I wait for her sleep meds to kick in
before I leave for home and a futile attempt at respite.

I have lost track of the days.
I know she will not last long.
Hope has slipped from my vocabulary.
My emotions have no center, my love has no focus;
Although I have never loved her so much.
I am filled with remorse--If only we could time travel back…
She is still physically strong and pulls up on the trapeze.

We live together in this circus, yet she still smiles through her
hip pain, smiles under the itch of the nasal oxygen tube.

These smiles belie that she hangs on to her bed
like a life preserver, like the last island in the storm.
Hangs on to me, embraces me for the last time,
over and over again and this goes on and on.
When this will end, I do not know.
Her pain has not been erased and like clockwork
I await her next anxiety attack, do what I can do
through love and all the strength I have
to face together the death that must come.

Soon.

The Lost Brother

For Scott Andrew Eret: b. August 6, 1965, d. August 6, 1965

Stillborn, you will never know
The dusty feel of playgrounds,
The Elysium of barefoot energy
Spent upon the park's grass.
Sometimes I can feel your umbilical cord
Tightening around my throat,
When the August air is humid with anxiety,
And someone is weeping over your coffin,
No larger than a violin case.

Scott, today you could smell the bacon burning
In the early spring air, hear
The lawnmower whining and smell
The freshly mown grass.
Other children skip and scream across it,
Playing out their hours in mortal bliss,
Pure wonder gleaming in their eyes.

Did you hear the green-masked men trying
To spank you, not for being naughty,
But to bring life back into your body,
Which turned blue after exiting the womb?
You would have been the youngest brother
And I would have been your oldest brother.
I could have shown you how to spiral
Punts into the eye of the sun,
Or we could have trapezeed like Tarzan
Down limb to limb

On the blossoming backyard apple tree.
I do not know many prayers,
None that would bring you back
From the grave I have never seen,
Weeded over and lost in Hammond, Indiana.
I think of the many hours moving
Slowly like long boxcars of freight trains
That pass the graveyard
Where they stop to the crash of their couplings,
Then lurch forward and rumble past the elm trees
And that final sound of the iron gate clanging shut,
The minute hand sweeping away your sacred breath
As the birds go mad with song
Near the river.